Addressing Matters of the Heart

Getting to the Root of Relational Distress

Lei Ross, PsyD

MW MEDIA
PORTLAND

Published in the United States by MW Media, LLC, Portland, Oregon

ISBN: 978-0-9907806-8-7 (pbk.)

Table of Contents

Dedication

This book is dedicated to my beloved husband, David, who has always been supportive of my endeavors, but more importantly, has been used by God to help me see the beauty of God's design for marriage. Married life has been filled with more joy than I could have ever imagined as a result of him. Je t'aime!

Introduction

Let me start off by saying that I am absolutely terrible when it comes to taking care of plants. I enjoy having them around. I enjoy looking at them. I enjoy how they can bring life to a seemingly stale and sterile space. Yet, for some reason I am completely inept when it comes to taking care of them.

Throughout the years many people have given me various types of plants from indoor bamboo plants to cactuses thinking that this was "the one" plant that I would not end up killing. Sadly, I have unintentionally ended the lives of many plants, all of which I had every intention of keeping around.

I have often told people that I just don't have a "green thumb." However, when I looked more closely at these experiences, I realized that saying, "I don't have a green thumb" is merely an excuse. An excuse? Yes, an excuse for the fact that I don't have the desire to take the time to learn anything about the needs of the plants I was given. What factors were necessary for each of them to grow? How much water and sunlight did they need? Where was the best spot for them, inside or outside of the house? Did they require any fertilizer? What signs were indications of overwatering or underwatering?

Instead of seeking out information to answer these questions, I based how to care for them on my oversimplified notion that they just needed to be watered every day. I honestly wasn't a good caretaker, as I was not willing to learn about the specific needs of each plant. I could have taken better care of these plants, however that was a commitment I obviously wasn't willing to make. If that were the case, I would have invested in them just as I would with a relationship I valued.

This is essentially the same with our hearts. In Proverbs 4:23 we are instructed to "Keep your heart with all vigilance, for from it flow the springs of life." We need to properly tend to our hearts so that they grow, produce, and bear fruit. How is this done? Psalm 119:9-12 answers this by saying:

> "How can a young man keep his way pure? By guarding it according to your word. With my whole heart I seek you; let me not wander from your commandments! I have stored up your word in my heart, that I might not sin against you. Blessed are you, O LORD; teach me your statutes!"

Our hearts soak up everything they are exposed to through each of our senses. This is why we need to guard our hearts. Just as we know that consuming junk food is not beneficial for our health, the same applies with our hearts as well. The nutrient-rich food of the Word of God is what we are called to feed our hearts with. Immersing our hearts in Scripture contributes to the life and vitality of our hearts. This prevents them from growing cold, hardened by pain and rejection, overridden by weeds, and yielding bad fruit that is only worthy of being discarded.

It's easy to read God's Word and simply give lip service to the concepts. There are many individuals who are well versed in what the Bible says. The real question is whether they have allowed God's Word to be their guide in all aspects of their life. Isaiah makes note of this in chapter 29 verse 13 which says:

> And the Lord said: "Because this people draw near with their mouth and honor me with their lips, while their hearts are far from me, and their fear of me is a commandment taught by men."

While feeding our hearts with God's Word is vital, we must also digest it, allow it to guide our thinking and decision-making, and direct our actions. This is why addressing matters of the heart is critical in our spiritual walk as Christians, but also in all of our relationships.

This became all the more apparent to me when I was working as a school administrator at a small Christian school. I had the task of developing a disciplinary plan that would be carried out by all the staff at the school. The methodology had to be clear so that the staff, students, and parents understood the expectations and parameters and so discipline could be consistently administered when necessary.

This process led me to speak with numerous school administrators from across the country, as well as parents who were homeschooling their children. I spent a lot of time studying the behaviors of the children who attended our church. As you may have guessed, the ones who caught my attention were those children who were not only well-behaved, but those who exercised sound decision making and engaged well with others of varying ages from youngsters to the oldest adults.

My discussions with their parents led to a common thread: they all focused on addressing the matters of their children's hearts when they exercised discipline. A common resource used among these families was Ginger Hubbard's book *Don't Make Me Count to Three!* and a booklet she wrote entitled *Wise Words for Moms* that was designed to assist parents with identifying the heart issue the child was struggling with based on the behavior they exhibited and how to address this from a biblical perspective. This transformed the way I looked at discipline as I was able to incorporate what I learned through my psychological background and reconcile it with God's word. Not only did I witness how effective it was, I saw how it provided students with the opportunity to examine the root of their behavior and how to correct it through the use of Scripture and modeling.

You may be wondering, "What does this have to do with marriage?" Hang in there and keep reading!! I need to lay the foundation for why this is so important, and I will eventually make the connection for you.

The Results of Relational Distress

The problems we are surrounded by today are the result of relational distress. You don't have to look far to see how much society has been impacted by it. People simply do not know how to cope with unpleasant emotions, such as anger, frustration, sadness, and disappointment in healthy ways. No longer do they see God as the source of truth, comfort, and peace. As a result, individuals struggle to find ways to handle problems and the unpleasant emotions that are associated with them on their own and are inclined to act out based on how they feel. This results in a host of problematic behaviors, from sadness, low frustration tolerance, blaming, anger, substance use, different forms of abuse and violence, and overt acting out behaviors.

Not sure of what I am talking about? Hopefully the following examples will help you see just how prevalent the matter is.

Have you ever witnessed road rage? You know what I am talking about, those drivers who are so impatient and indignant that they feel impelled to let you know just how much you have upset them through verbal assaults or impolite physical gestures when they don't like the way you or other people drive. In 2011 Patti Neighmond wrote an article entitled, "Road Rage: A Symptom of Much More Than Bad Traffic?" and described the following:

> The term road rage was coined in Los Angeles – a city long known for its epic freeway jams. Mike Shen got a taste of how bad it can get shortly after moving to L.A., when a woman viciously tailgated him on the freeway.
>
> "She got so angry that she started pacing me to my right," Shen says. "She wasn't looking at the road, she was literally yelling — out the window — racial epithets at the top of her lungs."

Countless examples such as this have led me to conclude that exercising frustration tolerance and self-control are no longer valued. We don't learn to live with frustration, instead we act upon it.

When you look at what gets covered in the media, the headlines often highlight people who cannot seem to control their anger. Anyone who goes to the grocery store is treated to a variety of publications that keep us all informed of the latest celebrity feuds, relationship break-ups, divorces, etc. Society seems to be enthralled by character assassinations held in the public arena and the media feeds into this by giving us more of it.

Social media is another area where we see the prevalence of emotional outbursts. Dockray (2015) stated:

For many of us, Facebook fights are a part of daily life. A 2012 Pew study found that 15% of adults and 22% of teens had engaged in an interaction on the site that resulted in a friendship ending. Three percent of adults and 8% of teens said that fighting on the website had led to fighting in real life.

Lane (2014) added,

Talking about someone behind his back isn't new, and neither is doing it in a place where he can hear it. Naturally, this prime method of passive-aggressive behavior has translated to social media — through the sub-post.

Lane gave the following examples:

After eight months together you go and cheat on me with that kid??? Whatever then…#swerve

Can't believe I wasted eight months of my life on that girl. Soooooo done with this

These are examples of short posts that can be quite damaging. However, there are individuals who feel justified in retaliating against others when they have been wronged and use social media as a platform to convey to the world just how badly they have been hurt. In the process of typing out a rant of what they've experienced, they attempt to solicit sympathy from others to provide further justification to themselves for their actions. They deem it necessary to let the world know they are "defriending" someone or post a long narrative giving a detailed account of the horrors of what they've been subjected to. They do not think twice about the kind of impact it will have on the target of their anger. In fact, they revel in seeing their prey being destroyed. With the frequency in which people destroy one another in the public domain, it can be concluded that society's apathy for attempting to bring an end to such conduct is equated with the condoning of this behavior.

Fascinatingly, this very same behavior can turn a once-comfortable work environment into a hostile one. If you have worked long enough, it is likely that you have come across a coworker that is known for being incredibly negative and critical of others, or the coworker that blames others for their shortcomings. Lea McLeod (2018) talked about these types of coworkers in her blog "How to Deal With the 5 Most Negative Types of Co-Workers."

> Victims blame others for their circumstances. Have you ever heard someone say the boss was out to get him or her? Victim. How about the person who blamed a missed deadline on the guys in accounting who "didn't get the report to me on time?" Victim.

> Co-workers with a victim syndrome constantly complain about everything bad that's happening in their lives. What's worse, they don't believe they have any ownership or control of the situation, so in their eyes, everything is being done to them. They often suspect there's some huge universal conspiracy that is firmly rooted against their success. And they love to talk about it.

Their melodrama and rants can go on and on. There is never an end to the number of things they can find to complain about. These coworkers can drain every last bit of energy left in you.

On the other end of the spectrum are those who struggle with a sense of worthlessness and emptiness. Their behaviors tend to be more self-directed and self-destructive. This is not to say that their conduct doesn't have an impact on others. While their actions are intended on addressing some sort of emotional void, they can be toxic to those around them. To fill the void, they engage in overindulgent and addictive behaviors. When we hear of addictive behaviors, we often think of drug and alcohol abuse and overlook other harmful vices such as sexual addictions, compulsive spending, gambling, and overindulgence in food or extreme food restriction, such as binge/purge eating disorders.

What? Overindulgence in food is an addictive behavior? Here's an excerpt from a *New York Times* article written by Jane Brody (2007).

> I learned where the few all-night mom-and-pop shops were located so I could pick up the evening's supply on my way home from work. Then I would spend the night eating nonstop, first something sweet, then something salty, then back to sweet, and so on. A half-gallon of ice cream was only the beginning. I was capable of consuming 3,000 calories at a sitting. Many mornings I awakened to find partly chewed food still in my mouth.

Obviously, the list of overindulgent and addictive behaviors doesn't stop here, but hopefully you get the picture.

All of these examples can trace their roots back to some form of relational distress. Given that every one of us can say that we have observed or experienced at least one of them, it serves as evidence of just how widespread the unhealthy outcome of relational distress is.

Now let me answer the question: how is this connected with marriage? Well, when you think about it, we are all capable of responding in inappropriate ways, especially when we allow our feelings to dictate our actions. We can easily become susceptible to behaving in the same manner as previously described when our buttons are pushed. The unfortunate reality is that in a marriage, it is our spouse that ends up being hit with the brunt of our distress.

No matter what type of a family a person comes from, each individual will experience disappointment and frustration at some point in life. How you deal with it is the key, as no one gets through life without experiencing some type of failure or distress. Jesus certainly didn't have it easy, and so we shouldn't expect to either (read about it in 1 Peter 4:12-16, Acts 14:22, Matthew 10:22).

Our approach to coping with difficulties stems from what we've been exposed to in our own families. If we haven't learned how to examine our hearts in the midst of emotional turmoil, we will be relegated to acting out in unbecoming ways. Therefore, it behooves all of us to examine the condition of our hearts and prevent our emotions from dictating our actions.

What Does Your Heart Say?

Romans 3:23 says, "for all have sinned and fall short of the glory of God."

The verse points out that we all have inherited a sin nature, which is the sin that has been passed down through the generations going all the way back to Adam. As a result, there is no one person that is good. We can engage in a host of good acts, but that does not make us good as far as the standards that God has set defining what good is.

In fact, Christians can be quite skilled at both doing good and looking good. From outward appearances, one may think that many Christians "have it together" and that good behavior just comes naturally. However, from the outside we can't see the person's heart, thus we don't know what is driving the behavior. Is their service done out of love and reverence for the Lord and a genuine compassion for those being served? Or, is it because they desire a pat on the back, recognition for what they've done, or to be in the limelight? If we can start articulating what is bound up in our hearts and what exactly is compelling us to act, we can take a step toward releasing any misplaced allegiances and experiencing the joy that God intends for us through the act of obedience.

Luke 6:45 says, "The good person out of the good treasure of his heart produces good, and the evil person out of his evil treasure produces evil, for out of the abundance of the heart his mouth speaks."

We see that this verse points out that our thoughts, words, and conduct stem from the condition of our hearts. So, if what we think, do, and say are the result of the condition of the heart, what does our heart say?

The reason this question is so important when it comes to marriage is because we are often driven by our hearts to do both good and bad things. This begs the question, "How is this playing out in your marriage?"

We all have ideas on how things should be, what they should look like, how things should be done, etc. Our expectations may or may not be reasonable. When our spouse behaves in a way that does not meet our expectations, it can evoke irritation, frustration, and anger in us. This may in turn result in responses that are not as loving or warm.

And yet, as Christians we are called to exercise self-control and to respond in love. How do we do that? Well, before we can exercise self-control and respond in love, we need to examine the condition of our own heart and look at the parts of ourselves that we typically avoid as they bring to light the ugliness that we do our best to conceal. Once we have identified the sin, we can begin modifying our thought process by putting on the mindset of Christ and allowing God's word to dictate our thought life and direct our steps.

Will this be hard? Of course it will! We have to honestly evaluate ourselves separate and apart from our circumstances. Without making the effort to take a look inside our hearts, we will forever be at the mercy of our rollercoaster of emotions and be subject to directing inappropriate, and possibly hurtful responses toward others, including our spouse.

How Do I See What's Really in My Heart?

To develop the skill of discerning the condition of your own heart, you need to cultivate an understanding of the nature of the internal conflict that is held in your heart and expressed in your outward behavior.

To illustrate this point, let's look at how Jesus addressed sinful conduct. It would have been easy for him to say, "Stop that!" or "Quit it!" Nevertheless, an astute observer recognizes that although you can tell a person to stop a behavior, the behavior will eventually resurface if you don't address the cause of the behavior itself.

Sometimes people engage in behaviors merely because they are on autopilot. Time after time they have responded to certain situations in the same way. As a result, it has become a "natural" response pattern for them. They no longer contemplate responding in any other way, they merely respond. It's almost like an instinctive response pattern.

Jesus's focus was not on the behavior itself, but on the conflict within the person's heart. If you look at what's on the surface, all you see is the behavior. Instead, Jesus dug deeper into the person's heart and unearthed the condition of the person's heart through a series of introspective questions and statements.

This is illustrated in Matthew Chapter 19 Verses 16-26:

> And behold, a man came up to him, saying, "Teacher, what good deed must I do to have eternal life?" And he said to him, "Why do you ask me about what is good? There is only one who is good."

Let's stop here for a minute. Jesus answers the man's question with a question followed by a statement of fact. He references that there is only one who is good: God. Jesus's comment also led the young man down the path to see Himself (Jesus) as God, the only one who is good. Therefore, whatever answer He gives to the man's question is authoritative and can be trusted to be accurate. If this doesn't cause you to pause and think for a moment, then it's about time you stopped to contemplate the gravity of this statement. In fact, you need to start training yourself to pause and absorb God's word more, as that is what's required to make lasting changes to a conflicted heart.

Jesus's words *should* cause all of us to pause, for when you compare yourself to a holy, righteous, pure, and perfect God, you don't just fall short, but you don't even qualify to be in the ranking on the scale of goodness! To think that eternal life is the result of something you can do is foolish and delusional thinking. No matter how good you think you are or how many thoughtful random acts of kindness you have done in your life, they will not gain you entrance into God's eternal kingdom.

Let's continue on with the account,

> "If you would enter life, keep the command-
> ments." He said to him, "Which ones?" And
> Jesus said, "You shall not murder, You shall not
> commit adultery, You shall not steal, You shall not
> bear false witness, Honor your father and mother,
> and, You shall love your neighbor as yourself."
> The young man said to him, "All these I have
> kept. What do I still lack?"

Jesus does not use the man's response as an opportunity to challenge whether or not he kept these commandments. However, the man's response exposes a sense of pride and self-righteousness as it insinuates that he is not deficient in any way for he has done all that was commanded of him.

There are a couple of hypotheses for the young man's answer.

Hypothesis #1: The young man did not know that our good conduct does not result in automatic entry into God's kingdom.

Hypothesis #2: The young man may have adhered to all the commandments, yet did not realize that the motive behind his actions is more important than the act itself.

Doing a good deed for the sake of checking off a box to say you've completed the task is very different from doing something with the desire to honor and worship God through reverent obedience to His commandments, and to do so with a joyful heart. In other words, the young man may have missed the spirit behind the intent of the law and did things with the wrong intent of heart.

The account continues…

> Jesus said to him, "If you would be perfect, go,
> sell what you possess and give to the poor, and you

will have treasure in heaven; and come, follow me." When the young man heard this he went away sorrowful, for he had great possessions.

Jesus's invitation to follow him came at what the young man thought was too high of a price to pay. Despite doing his best to follow God's commandments, it appears that Hypothesis #2 provides a better explanation for his actions: his heart was more invested in his earthly possessions versus the treasure of eternal life.

It wasn't necessary for Jesus to point out whether the young man kept the commandments, nor was it necessary for him to point out that the young man valued his material possessions over the kingdom of God. Jesus merely used questions and statements to guide the young man into recognizing the conflict in his heart and also gave him a solution to release him from the grip that sin had on his heart.

This process of highlighting the condition of one's heart is not unique to just the young man. Jesus does this with us as well through the truths spelled out in His word. Our primary obstacle is that we often don't refer to God's word to guide us so that we steer clear of allowing our depraved hearts from taking the lead. Or, if we are presented with God's word, we don't allow it to permeate the hard exterior of our hearts and we permit our corrupt hearts to proceed anyway.

Fortunately, it doesn't have to be that way. To ensure that our hearts remain malleable and receptive to God's word, we must diligently challenge our heart's perverse inclinations with God's word no matter how strongly our hearts want to go in a contrary direction. We must step back and shift our focus from our situation and the responses of others to doing a thorough examination of our hearts.

There are a number of clues that will help us determine

which of God's truth(s) apply when it comes to understanding the condition of our hearts.

Clue #1: Behavior

The first clue, which should be the most obvious, is your behavior. What was your response to the situation? The first clue gives you a sense of your response pattern when you feel provoked, hurt, offended, or embarrassed in some way.

- Did you yell at our spouse?

- Did you make a snide remark?

- Did you talk over your spouse when he was trying to talk?

- Did you simply ignore and/or walk away from your spouse?

- Did you refuse to help your spouse when she needed assistance?

- Did you try to inflict harm by throwing something or physically restraining your spouse?

Clue #2: Words

When you reflect on your behavior, take a moment to look at your specific response pattern. What words did you use? Oftentimes people will say that they utter the "first words" that come to mind. There is something to be said about those first words. Couples often know, or at least have a sense, that there are certain words, phrases, or topics that can easily set off our spouse. These biting words/comments are selected (consciously or unconsciously, it doesn't matter) because you know they will evoke the response you desire for the following purposes:

- To hurt your spouse

- To embarrass your spouse

- For your spouse to feel shame and guilt

- For your spouse to feel like an utter failure and is thus responsible for all disagreements

- For your spouse to feel belittled and deserving of whatever you dish out

- To intimidate your spouse and let her know who has the upper hand in the situation

Clue #3: Desired Reaction

Next, look at what you hoped to accomplish through your behavior and words (Clue #1 and Clue #2). Our actions and words convey how we feel, but as it was stated in Clue #2, they are often used to provoke a desired reaction as well. These desired reactions are attempts to exert control over the situation and our spouse, albeit in very hurtful and dysfunctional ways. The following are some common examples of desired reactions when conflict in our heart takes over:

- You threw your keys at the wall in a fit of rage to evoke fear in your wife

- You walked away from your husband as he was talking to convey that you had enough and had no interest in continuing to talk

- You reminded your wife of her failed attempts to lose the pregnancy weight in hopes that by shaming and belittling her, she would shut down the argument

- You brought up the time your husband was passed over for a promotion to remind him of his past failures and illustrate why your marriage is riddled with problems

- You blamed your wife for your anger to ensure she knew she was the cause of the problems in the marriage

- You rolled your eyes and turned your back to your husband whenever he spoke to convey how foolish you think his opinions are

- Whenever your wife tried to engage in a discussion about the disagreements you were having, you stonewalled her and tried to get her to disengage by giving her the silent treatment or short, one-word answers

What is most intriguing about our actions towards others is that it is more of a reflection of how we feel and the emotional conflict contained in our hearts than the feelings we attempt to evoke from our spouse. Of course, actions that convey disregard and contempt for our spouse will result in a host of unpleasant reactions and have long-lasting effects. The very thing you are trying to evoke in your spouse should be an indication of the conflict taking place within you.

So, for example, if you find yourself pointing out every single flaw and mistake your wife has made over the course of your marriage, what your actions really convey is a sense of your own personal failures and shortcomings. In fact, that is what all of the heart conditions have in common: they reflect fear associated with feeling devalued, unimportant, unlovable, flawed, and unworthy. The saying "misery loves company" is so true when our motive is for our spouse to get dragged into the same muddy pit we are in because it is never fun to be alone in those moments of despair.

This is what it all boils down to: ask yourself, "What do I hope to gain from aggravating my spouse?" Whatever your answer is reflects the conflict (or better known as sin) in your heart. Once you know the conflict in your heart, you can confront it with God's word. What does Scripture say about the bitterness in your heart? The anger you harbor toward your spouse? The desire you have to retaliate and take revenge out on your spouse?

Once you know what God's word says about the conflict in your heart, you can start to see things from God's perspective and not merely your own, and begin taking steps to alter your relational response pattern.

How to Use This Book

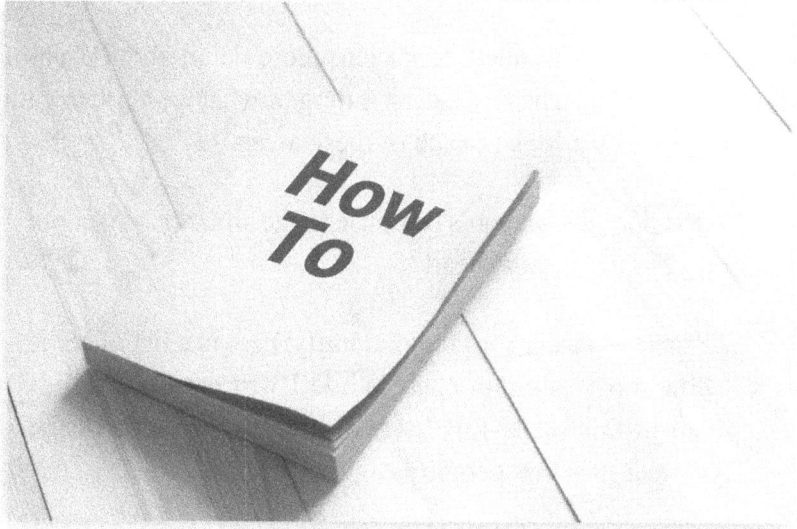

The rest of the book focuses on some of the common heart conditions that drive our problematic relational responses. I will share real-life stories of couples that I have worked with that describe many of these response patterns. Their names and some of the specific details have been changed to protect their identity. However, what their stories illustrate are some of the same struggles we each face when relational challenges arise.

Each chapter will start with a snapshot of a real-life struggle that a couple has experienced. This will be followed by the same series of three questions and issues to consider for self-reflection so that we can examine the heart condition that the person is struggling with and how to address it. They are as follows:

1. What does the person's response to the situation say about the condition of his heart?

2. What does God's word say about this heart condition?

3. How does the person's conduct need to change in order to be in line with God's word?

4. Issues to consider for self-reflection

Let me take a moment to go into more detail about each of them so you have a better understanding of what we hope to gain by taking a closer look at each of these areas.

1. What does the person's response to the situation say about the condition of his heart?

   To make it easier for you to identify, here is a list of some of the most common ones. While I will not cover all of them in this book, this list will give you an idea of the typical issues that people struggle with.

   - Aggravating Others

   - Anger

   - Anxiety/Worry

   - Arguing/Quarreling

   - Blame Shifting

   - Complaining

   - Desire for Revenge

   - Despair

   - Discontentment/Bitterness

   - Envy

- Fear

- Greed

- Lying

- Pride

- Selfishness

- Slander/Defamation of Character/Tearing Down Others

2. What does God's word say about this heart condition?

Although there will be discussion of what Scripture says about the specific heart condition, it is my hope that you will see this as an opportunity to do your own research and reflect on it for yourself. There are a number of easy ways to find out what Scripture says about the specific issue if you are unsure. Some bibles have a topical index in the back that allows you to search for verses by topic.

If your bible does not have a topical index, there are free sources available online. BibleGateway.com, BibleStudy-Tools.com, and Christianity.com are websites that have a search function and list the verses that are applicable to the search topic.

On the other hand, if you want an actual hardcopy book, John Kruis has written three different books entitled *Quick Scripture Reference for Counseling, Quick Scripture Reference for Counseling Men*, and *Quick Scripture Reference for Counseling Women*. Each book has an array of topics and Scripture references to assist with resolving specific issues.

Once you have read through the Scripture references for the specific heart-related conflict that the character in the story is struggling with, reflect on the following:

- What does Scripture say about the impact this heart condition can have on the person and those around them?

- Next, look at it from a personal perspective. How does your understanding and belief of God's truth regarding this heart condition line up with God's word?

- Does your understanding and belief about this truth need to change in order to be in line with God's word?

3. How does the person's conduct need to change in order to be in line with God's word?

To answer this question requires that we examine the following areas for each story:

- *Change related to the specific heart condition*

  God's word has a prescription on how to address each of these heart conditions. An easy way to look at this is that God is calling us to do the exact opposite of the sinful heart condition. For example, the change required for a heart consumed with anger is to be slow to anger.

- *Confession*

Proverbs 28:13 says, "Whoever conceals his transgressions will not prosper, but he who confesses and forsakes them will obtain mercy." God is acutely aware of all of our wrongdoings, so the importance of confession isn't for us to inform God of our sin. Rather, confession is an opportunity for us to recognize and acknowledge the sin plaguing our heart and how it blindsides us from seeing how our actions hinder our relationship with God and others. The saying "confession is good for the soul" reflects the truth that when we declare our heart condition to God and others, it diminishes the power that our sin has on us and our response patterns. This frees us from being in bondage to its grip and brings relief to our tormented soul.

Through confession we take responsibility for our inappropriate response patterns. This paves the way for taking steps to move forward in changing our relational patterns. Since no one, including our spouse, is able to read our mind, we have to be willing to verbally communicate what is going on inside of us, and confession is the mechanism that allows for this to occur. This type of dialogue can open the door for further discussion regarding obtaining help to remain accountable with the changes you are looking to institute.

- *Return good for evil*

  Romans 12:21 says, "Do not be overcome by evil, but overcome evil with good." At this point you have a choice to make. You can either continue to allow your mistakes to pile up one after the other until you find that you have created a disastrous mess, or you can make the choice to turn your conduct around, which would be in line with Romans 12:21. We must remember that it is not anyone else's responsibility to change but our own. So, be the one to take the first step to pick up the pieces and restore the relationship.

- *Self-reflection*

  Self-reflection is a vital part of instituting change. There are a number of triggers that set people off, hence it is important to identify what those triggers are for you. This process of self-reflection will require replaying troublesome situations so that they can be examined more closely. As unpleasant as this may be, it is necessary so that we can begin to identify our personal response pattern to unfavorable situations.

  Sometimes it is hard for us to see our own faults, thus we may need help from a friend or trained professional to pinpoint specific triggers that contribute to our response pattern so they can be properly addressed. Don't allow fear or shame to prevent you from seeking help.

Remember that such an emotional response to seeking help is what impedes people from obtaining help that allows for growth.

Ephesians 4:31-32 says, "Let all bitterness and wrath and anger and clamor and slander be put away from you, along with all malice. Be kind to one another, tenderhearted, forgiving one another, as God in Christ forgave you." Therefore, it would be wise to learn how to address triggers that provoke engaging in sinful acts so that your demeanor reflects a heart that is kind, tenderhearted, and forgiving toward your spouse and others.

4. Issues to consider for self-reflection

This book is to be used for self-reflection. Personalize the questions by replacing the character's name with your own. Ask yourself the very same questions:

- Have I experienced this particular heart condition? If so, how do I respond?

- Knowing what God's word says about this heart condition, what do I need to change in order to be in line with His word?

Use the section in the back of the book entitled "Addressing Matters of My Heart: A Self-Reflection Journal" to help you put your thoughts together. I encourage you to use this as a guide so that you can personalize and apply the material to your life. My hope is for you to actively use the concepts in this book to bring about transformation in your relationships. This can only take place when a person puts the concepts into action. So, use the journal in this book to facilitate change in your relational response patterns.

It is noteworthy to keep in mind that as fallible human beings, we make mistakes. We may get it right one day and then mess up the next. It is easy to fall prey to feeling guilty and burdened by our failures. Beware of allowing your mistakes to define you and leave you feeling insecure, inferior, and defective.

Journaling can help you keep an appropriate perspective and assist with identifying patterns related to the condition of your heart. Regular review of your journal entries can help you track the progress being made and align your heart and life with God's word.

Every time we defy God's word through our inappropriate response patterns, He blesses us with unmeasurable grace by giving us the opportunity to learn from our mistakes. Will you seize the opportunity or will you allow your old destructive patterns to persist? Our failures serve as further justification for our need for Jesus. So, allow Him to be your guide and strength through this process, for no one can make these changes alone.

Heart Condition:
Anger

As mentioned in the previous chapter, the stories used in this book are based on real accounts of couples that I have worked with. Their names and some specific details have been changed to protect their identity. These stories will be used to illustrate the conditions of the heart and how we can get our hearts back in line with God. So, take a minute to put yourself in their shoes and let's examine the various conflicts of the heart together.

> *John had a very stressful day at work and couldn't wait for it to end. All he could think about was for 5:00 p.m. to roll around so he could head home. Unbeknownst to him, there was a car accident not far from work that caused a major backlog*

on the freeway. His normal twenty-minute drive turned into an hour and a half of sitting in gridlock traffic. With each passing minute John grew even more tired, grouchy, and famished. He was relieved when he finally made it home. However, when he walked in the door, he found that his wife was just starting to make dinner. John became infuriated with Jane and couldn't contain his anger. He exploded and yelled, "I'm an hour and a half late and you still haven't cooked dinner?! All I wanted was to come home to a meal after a lousy day at work and you can't even do that!"

What does John's response to the situation say about the condition of his heart?

First, let's identify the conflict in John's heart that is driving his behavior. (Refer to the list of heart conditions from the previous chapter if you need assistance). While there are many things that can be targeted, let's start with anger.

Throughout the day John seemed to be contending with frustrating situations, work stress, dealing with unexpected traffic, fatigue, and hunger. Although we can understand how the culmination of these factors could lead to anger, explosive outbursts are not obligatory responses to anger.

Anger is often the result of feeling threatened. The perception of being threatened may not be real, but when a person experiences humiliation, a sense of injustice, danger to self or others, or being unable to control one's circumstances, it is not uncommon for a person to become defensive and do whatever is necessary to protect oneself from a real or perceived threat.

What does God's word say about anger?

Scripture has quite a bit to say about anger. Nevertheless, before we move forward, we need to address the fact that anger (or indignation) can be deemed as righteous when the target of our anger is what angers God. It should anger us when others are being violated or when harm is being inflicted on others through the means of abortion, child abuse, pornography, racism, sex slave trafficking, etc. However, the anger we experience should not spur us on to engaging in further evil acts. God's righteous anger should provoke us to respectfully advocate for those who do not have a voice or are unable to make their needs known.

With that being said, let's look at what the Bible says about anger and the importance of being able to properly manage it.

We started off with talking about righteous anger. However, when our pride is the cause of anger, it is no longer righteous, but sinful. In James 1:20 it says, "for the anger of man does not produce the righteousness of God." When our pride takes over, it prevents us from conducting ourselves in a humble manner. It inhibits any desire and ability to see things from any other perspective but our own. Instead, we are determined to point fingers at others and pin the blame on them for the hurt and dis-appointment we experience.

While angry outbursts may initially give us the satisfaction of feeling vindicated, we must recognize that when we give in to our anger and let it run amuck, it destroys our relationship with our spouse, others, and, as Galatians 5:19-21 says, with God as well:

> Now the works of the flesh are evident: sexual immorality, impurity, sensuality, idolatry, sorcery, enmity, strife, jealousy, fits of anger, rivalries, dissensions, divisions, envy, drunkenness, orgies,

and things like these. I warn you, as I warned you before, that those who do such things will not inherit the kingdom of God.

Unrestrained anger prevents a person from being able to calm down and be soothed. Rather, it enslaves its victim to the clutches of bitterness, which leads to rivalries, dissensions, divisions, holding on to grudges, and the destruction of relational bonds. This is in direct contradiction to Ephesians 4:26-27 which says, "Be angry and do not sin; do not let the sun go down on your anger, and give no opportunity to the devil." The more we allow our anger to get a foothold in our hearts and minds, the more inclined we are to act on it whenever it arises, and the more we become ruled by it.

How does John's conduct need to change in order to be in line with God's word?

Slow to anger

Proverbs 29:11 says, "A fool gives full vent to his spirit, but a wise man quietly holds it back." James 1:19 also says, "Know this, my beloved brothers: let every person be quick to hear, slow to speak, slow to anger."

When we are upset, our initial inclination is to respond without thinking about the consequences of our actions. Scripture tells us that we need to take a minute when we find ourselves consumed with anger. Perhaps this is where the idea of counting before you speak when you are angry came from. It's quite intriguing to think that this practice has some biblical basis to it and was even used by Thomas Jefferson who said, "When angry, count to 10 before you speak. If very angry, a hundred," (Sorgen, 2018).

Knowing this, John could have taken time to evaluate how

he was feeling, assessed the situation, and prayed for godly wisdom on how to best manage his frustration so that he could calm down before he reacted. As we all know, the moment we say or do something, we can't take it back. So, let your actions and what comes out of your mouth be pleasing to God.

Confession

John could have taken a moment to confess his sin of anger to God, and prayed for God's help to be released from the control that anger had on him. During his time of confession, he could invite God to fill his mind with wisdom on how best to communicate with Jane in a calm and loving manner.

Just as John confessed to God that his heart was engulfed by anger, it would be wise for him to confess his sinful heart condition to Jane and ask for her forgiveness. This could help to bridge the gap in their ability to openly communicate as a couple that his behavior created.

Return good for evil

John completely blew it by yelling at Jane, but instead of leaving things in utter chaos he could have confessed, asked for forgiveness, and offered to help. The following are a few things John could have done to rectify the situation:

- John could have offered to help Jane get dinner ready by serving as her "sous chef" (e.g., get items out of the refrigerator and/or pantry, prepare the ingredients by measuring, cleaning, cutting items to be cooked, stir items that are being heated on the stove, etc.) or help to set the table, wash the dishes, etc.

- John could have tended to the children so that Jane

could finish getting dinner ready.

- John could have tried to change the mood of the evening by putting on some relaxing music or something he knows that Jane would enjoy.

- John could have gotten a few snack items out of the pantry, poured a glass of Jane's favorite beverage, and served it to her as she prepared dinner.

John could have done a number of things to not just "make up" for his explosive temper, but to actively change his response pattern while also taking steps to restore the relationship.

Self-reflection

To prevent verbal outbursts from occurring in the future, John has to learn to identify what serves as triggers for the anger he experiences. Anger is often the result of holding on to past hurts (e.g., rejection, losses, personal attacks), unmet irrational expectations, and personal faults we would rather cover up, which then get redirected at others. Knowing what his triggers are will help John become more self-aware when anger-provoking situations arise in the future.

Time for self-reflection

- Have I experienced the heart condition of anger? If so, how do I respond?

- Knowing what God's word says about anger, what do I need to change in order to be in line with God's word?

Heart Condition: Complaining

There are a number of heart conditions that cause us to respond in unsightly ways. In the previous chapter we looked at anger being the sin driving John's behavior. This time we will look at the same story and examine how another heart condition can contribute to the same or similar behavior.

> *John had a very stressful day at work and couldn't wait for it to end. All he could think about was for 5:00 p.m. to roll around so he could head home. Unbeknownst to him, there was a car accident not far from work that caused a major backlog on the freeway. His normal twenty-minute drive turned into an hour and a half of sitting in*

gridlock traffic. With each passing minute John grew even more tired, grouchy, and famished. He was relieved when he finally made it home. However, when he walked in the door, he found that his wife was just starting to make dinner. John became infuriated with Jane and couldn't contain his anger. He exploded and yelled, "I'm an hour and a half late and you still haven't cooked dinner?! All I wanted was to come home to a meal after a lousy day at work and you can't even do that!"

What does John's response to the situation say about the condition of his heart?

One of the many sins driving John's conduct is a heart consumed by complaining, hence he was angry that dinner was not ready when he arrived. Complaining often arises when we have our own preconceived notions of how things should be, according to us, of course. It is a self-centered response, as it doesn't take anything into account except our personal expectations regardless of whether or not they are irrational.

From John's perspective, Jane is not demonstrating love and appreciation and thus he feels justified in complaining. It is an irrational jump to make, and yet it almost makes sense in a distorted way if you have unrealistic expectations of your spouse (e.g., you believe that your spouse's role is to ensure your happiness and do everything to make your life enjoyable and comfortable) and how your spouse is to express love and to communicate appreciation (e.g., you believe that your spouse should instinctively know how to make your life comfortable without being told).

What does God's word say about complaining?

Philippians 2:14 says, "Do all things without grumbling or disputing, that you may be blameless and innocent, children of God without blemish in the midst of a crooked and twisted generation, among whom you shine as lights in the world." 1 Peter 4:9 adds, "Show hospitality to one another without grumbling."

Based on these verses, it appears that complaining, grumbling, and disputing are behaviors that are unbecoming of followers of Jesus Christ. Why? Because it reflects a worldly heart that is consumed with unfulfilled desires that eventually lead to envy and strife. If we are to shine as lights for Christ in this dark and corrupt world, we should be known for conduct that sets us apart from the world, not demeanor that the world can identify with.

Galatians 5:22-23 makes reference to the fruit of the Spirit being "love, joy, peace, patience, kindness, goodness, faithfulness, gentleness, self-control." Complaining prevents a person from being able to experience the fruit of the Spirit. When we are consumed by discontent, we are unable to experience the love, joy, and peace that God blesses us with regardless of our circumstances. Instead, a complainer glosses over God's blessings and zeroes in on those things that are unpleasant and objectionable.

James 1:2-4 says, "Count it all joy, my brothers, when you meet trials of various kinds, for you know that the testing of your faith produces steadfastness. And let steadfastness have its full effect, that you may be perfect and complete, lacking in nothing." Romans 8:28 adds, "And we know that for those who love God all things work together for good, for those who are called according to his purpose."

How is a complainer to experience joy in times of trial? How is a complainer able to see God's truth that He is working all things together, including times of suffering and struggle, for good? Read on to see how a complainer can change his attitude and mindset.

How does John's conduct need to change in order to be in line with God's word?

Heart of gratitude

We need to alter our thinking so that we aren't fixated on what we perceive to be shortcomings in life. The less time and energy we invest in something, the less consuming it will be. Having the right attitude and mindset is essential to making noted cognitive and perceptual changes. In this instance, being grateful and demonstrating thanks is contrary to complaining and is a biblical attitude to have.

In this scenario, John's attitude and words toward Jane do not convey that. Philippians 2:14 states that the Lord calls us to do everything without arguing and complaining. In John's situation, he needs to put aside his frustration and focus on what God desires of him (and all of His children), which is to have a thankful heart in all circumstances, even when dinner is not ready when he gets home, and put 1 Thessalonians 5:16-18 into action, which says, "Rejoice always, pray without ceasing, give thanks in all circumstances; for this is the will of God in Christ Jesus for you."

The moment that John recognized that complaining filled his heart, he could begin probing his actions and how they align with God's word regarding this heart condition. The following are some questions he could ask himself:

- "Are my words demonstrating the thankful heart that God desires for me to exhibit toward my wife?"

- "Are my actions exhibiting how thankful I am for the wife God has given me?"

- "Rather than complaining that dinner isn't ready, what can I be grateful for at this moment (e.g., safely getting home, a loving wife, a place to call home, etc.)?"

Taking a moment to reflect on your answers to similar questions when complaining takes hold of your heart forces you to see how you are in fact contributing to the exacerbation of the situation. No longer is it about Jane not getting dinner ready on time. It is about how John's conduct turned a situation that did not require a verbal outburst into a relational disaster.

Confession

John could have taken a moment to confess his struggles with complaining to God. In his confession to God, John could ask the Lord for help to see the blessings in his life rather than finding fault in everything. This could help him see the many things to be thankful for: having work, a car to transport him to and from work, safe travel home, the fact that he has a home, and that he is blessed with a wife who cares and tends to his needs.

By confessing to Jane that he allowed discontentment to blind him and asking for her forgiveness, John's transparency allows Jane an inside look into the struggles he feels defeated by and how she can support him. This could be a start for the couple to look at how their differences actually complement each other.

Return good for evil

As mentioned previously, having a heart of gratitude allows a person to break out of the rut of finding deficiencies in every situation. The following are ways that a complainer can demonstrate a heart of gratitude and be a blessing to their spouse rather than maintaining a dysfunctional pattern of complaining and criticizing.

- The moment that John experienced disappointment and frustration, he could have focused on being grateful that Jane was in the process of getting dinner ready and offered to help.

- Instead of being focused on how terrible of a day he had and how terrible his night was going, John could have taken the focus off himself and demonstrated compassion for his wife by asking Jane how her day went, as circumstances may have come up that prevented her from starting dinner as she originally planned.

- In line with this, John could have made efforts to bless Jane rather than seek for her to join him in his misery. This could be easily accomplished by saying things to encourage Jane, doing things to be helpful, showing affection, and going the extra mile to ensure that Jane knows that she is appreciated and that he loves and cares for her.

Self-reflection

John's struggle with complaining points to some significant issues. The first is the perception that we are "the center of the universe." When we find ourselves believing the delusion that "the world revolves around me," we can't help but be disappointed because no one will measure up to our unrealistic expectations. Why? Because there is no one else in this world exactly like you! While we may not necessarily think the world revolves around us, our responses and expectations seem to demonstrate otherwise.

The more significant issue that is brought out as a result of complaining is that it illustrates how forgetful we are about all that Jesus has done for us. Having a heart of gratitude should not be dependent on our circumstances, how much or little we possess, how great or mediocre our job is, whether our home is in a fantastic or ordinary neighborhood, whether we struggle with health issues or if we are in tip-top shape, etc. A heart of gratitude is inspired by the reality of all that God has done for us. The Lord extended an invitation to be adopted into His family, to be heirs to His kingdom, to be freed from the bondage to sin, to be given the gift of eternal life with Him, and this was all done at *His* expense, not ours. How easy it is to forget about the gift of deliverance from eternal damnation and His perfect daily provision when we have expectations of what our blessings should look like.

If you are a complainer like John, pause here to reflect on the cross and the price that was paid for you.

Time for self-reflection

- Have I experienced the heart condition of complaining? If so, how do I respond?

- Knowing what God's word says about complaining, what do I need to change in order to be in line with God's word?

Heart Condition:
Blame-Shifting

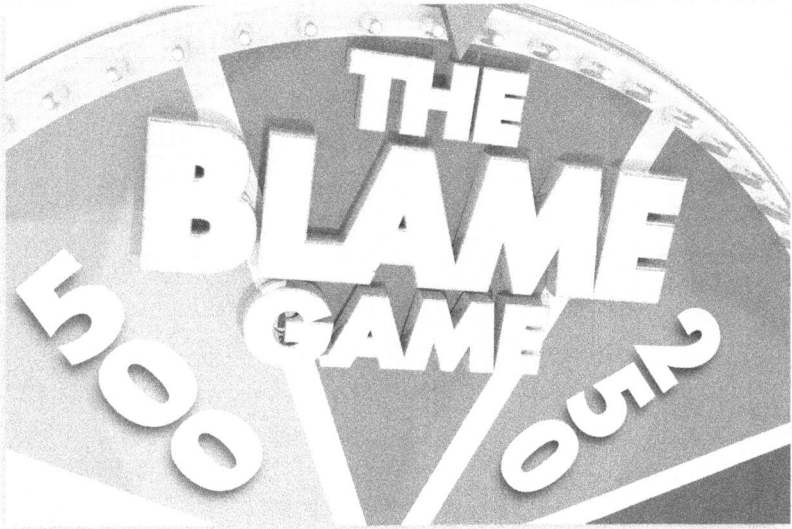

As we address matters of the heart, it forces us to take an honest look at what is really going on inside of us. None of us really wants to examine the condition of our hearts, as we simply want to believe that we are pretty good people, no matter what we think, say, or do. Despite what we think, Scripture continues to remind us that "The heart is deceitful above all things, and desperately wicked: who can know it?" (Jeremiah 17:9).

So far we have seen that in one scenario there are a number of heart conditions at play. It may seem redundant, but let's take another look at this same scenario that we've been examining in the past two chapters and see if there are other heart-related issues that need to be addressed.

John had a very stressful day at work and couldn't wait for it to end. All he could think about was for 5:00 p.m. to roll around so he could head home. Unbeknownst to him, there was a car accident not far from work that caused a major backlog on the freeway. His normal twenty-minute drive turned into an hour and a half of sitting in gridlock traffic. With each passing minute John grew even more tired, grouchy, and famished. He was relieved when he finally made it home. However, when he walked in the door, he found that his wife was just starting to make dinner. John became infuriated with Jane and couldn't contain his anger. He exploded and yelled, "I'm an hour and a half late and you still haven't cooked dinner?! All I wanted was to come home to a meal after a lousy day at work and you can't even do that!"

What does John's response to the situation say about the condition of his heart?

John's response reveals a very self-centered focus, which renders him incapable of taking into account anything pertaining to Jane. Her thoughts and feelings don't even make it onto John's radar because his focus is on himself, hence the possibility that she could have had just as bad a day didn't cross his mind.

In some ways we can understand why John was upset. He worked all day, he got stuck in traffic (which no one really cares for), and he was tired and hungry by the time he got home. A day like that could easily lead someone to become irritable and grouchy when things don't go as planned. After all, regardless of our circumstances, it should never serve as justification to blame someone else for the frustration we may experience. We need to take responsibility for how we are thinking and feeling and not project that onto others.

Have you ever caught yourself doing this? It is so much easier to "pass the buck" on to someone else so that we can "save face." Nevertheless, we have to take into consideration how this will impact the relationship with the person whom we are passing blame on to, which in this case is our spouse. How can we expect to have a relationship that grows in depth and trust when we act on our propensity to blame our spouse for our personal shortcomings?

What does God's word say about blame-shifting?

In the scenario we see John blaming Jane for his irritation and feels his explosive demeanor is justified. At the root of blame-shifting is pride, as we would rather be right and justified for our actions (regardless of what they may be) or viewed in a better light by others.

Proverbs 28:13 says, "Whoever conceals his transgressions will not prosper, but he who confesses and forsakes them will obtain mercy."

Not only will the person engaging in the blame-shifting not thrive and succeed, but neither will the marriage. Blame-shifting creates a rift that leads to distrust and animosity. However, if we carry out what the rest of the verse says (but he who confesses and forsakes them will obtain mercy), we can begin to trust one another more, as vulnerabilities and personal limitations are shared—not exploited.

Matthew 7:3-5 says,

> Why do you see the speck that is in your brother's

eye, but do not notice the log that is in your own
eye? Or how can you say to your brother, 'Let
me take the speck out of your eye,' when there is
the log in your own eye? You hypocrite, first take
the log out of your own eye, and then you will
see clearly to take the speck out of your brother's
eye.

How easy it is to find fault in others and yet be so inept at
recognizing that we, too, are bearers of sin. Before we point our
finger at someone for their indiscretions, we need to be willing
to examine our hearts and the motive driving our desire to assign
blame onto others. Are you highlighting the shortcomings of
your spouse because you want to deflect any focus on your own
insecurities and wrongdoings? Are you refusing to take responsibility for how your actions contribute to the problems you two
are experiencing because it is so much easier to see your partner
as the identified problem? It is time to check your heart!

How does John's conduct need to change in order to be in line with God's word?

Exercise humility

We should view humility as one of the most fundamental
characteristics of being a Christian, as our Savior, Jesus Christ
was the ultimate example of this. Despite being God in the flesh,
He did not put himself before others or expect special treatment.
Thus, in John's case, rather than giving himself permission to
discharge responsibility, he needed to exercise humility and take
responsibility for his own conduct. Instead of merely thinking
of himself, exercising humility requires that John take everyone
involved into consideration and critically consider how his
actions impact the familial dynamics.

Confession

It is easy to fall prey to exalting yourself above God, especially when you have tunnel vision and see yourself and your needs and desires as being more important than anything else. John needed to humble himself and confess to the Lord that he usurped God's rightful position and put himself first. John could have prayed for God to give him eyes to see the struggles of others, and for the desire to be involved in addressing their needs.

Rather than shifting blame to Jane, John could have exercised humility by confessing his sin to her. Open confession allows your spouse to see the *real* you—with your faults, shortcomings, quirkiness, and any "ugliness" that you may be afraid to reveal to anyone else. Remember that this is the person you have committed your life to. Even if sharing your vulnerabilities is a terrifying thought, imagine just how much the two of you can grow as you begin addressing these issues as a couple.

Return good for evil

A humble heart doesn't see oneself as more important than another and thus puts others before oneself. As a result, our actions are focused on meeting the needs of others. In line with having a humble heart is the recognition that some situations are merely annoyances. They don't necessarily require action on our part, nor are they worth investing our time and emotional energy, so we should simply let them go.

This is comparable to 1 Peter 4:8, which says, "Above all, keep loving one another earnestly, since love covers a multitude of sins." By letting go of these petty irritations, we prevent ourselves from getting worked up emotionally or unnecessarily reacting and eventually paying the consequences for poor choices.

Knowing this, here are a few things that John could have done:

- Take responsibility for allowing his emotional outburst and stress to Jane that she is not to blame for his inappropriate conduct.

- When John found himself consumed with irritation and wanted to place blame on someone/something for how he felt, he could have recognized that it was a petty annoyance that wasn't worth getting agitated over. Instead, he could have focused on what could be done at that very moment to make the night enjoyable for the whole family.

- The moment John felt irritated when he saw that dinner wasn't ready, he could have taken time to think about "removing the log from his eyes" before being quick to point out fault with Jane.

- As mentioned previously, John could have shifted his focus to finding out what he could do that would be helpful to Jane so that they could all enjoy dinner and the rest of the night together.

- John could have checked in with Jane to see how her night was going. Perhaps she was feeling overwhelmed with trying to quickly get dinner done now that he was home. John could have asked Jane if it would be easier for them to go out to eat or to get some food delivered.

Self-reflection

There are several factors that contribute to the tendency to blame others. Let's start with the desire to present an unblemished front and the tendency to avoid acknowledging one's flaws and failures.

If blame can be placed on someone else, not only are we off the hook, but it removes any reason for us to change, for who likes required change? It can also be a "useful" weapon of mass destruction that can be employed when we are in "attack mode" and desiring to hurt someone.

A third cause for blame- shifting occurs when we have faulty expectations of others. This leads to distorted perceptions of other's reactions and behaviors, poor judgment, and erroneous conclusions. In other words, we end up blaming people for things they didn't do, but rather for things that we've conjured up in our minds that they have done.

Regardless of which of these reasons trigger John's propensity to blame others, he needs to establish what is prompting his inappropriate responses.

Time for self-reflection

- Have I experienced the heart condition of blame-shifting? If so, how do I respond?

- Knowing what God's word says about blame-shifting, what do I need to change in order to be in line with God's word?

Heart Condition:
Arguing and Quarreling

The condition of our heart drives us to respond in a host of different ways. In the past chapters we examined how various heart conditions can manifest in one scenario. This time we are going to look at things from Jane's perspective, examine what heart condition is exhibited, and what we can do to get our heart better aligned with God's word.

> Jane found herself rushing to get dinner started after cleaning up the dreadful mess that was made when the kids knocked over a glass vase. Although she tried to quickly pick up all the pieces, she kept finding tiny sharp fragments in the most unsuspecting places. She barely got

things out of the refrigerator when John walked in the door and yelled, "I'm an hour and a half late and you still haven't cooked dinner?! All I wanted was to come home to a meal after a lousy day at work and you can't even do that!" Jane lashed back with, "If you're that hungry, why don't you cook your own food?!" and stormed out of the kitchen.

What does Jane's response to the situation say about the condition of her heart?

While John did not have to be so harsh with Jane, her response to John was not the most loving either. When we are hurt, especially when it seems to come out of nowhere, emotional buttons get pressed and vicious verbal attacks get launched. If our past did not provide opportunities to identify and process through our feelings, we will be inclined to respond instanta- neously without thought to how it will impact our spouse and the consequential backlash this will have on your relationship. As we see from this scenario, returning a verbal attack with more arguing and quarreling did not help the situation but aggravated an already tense moment.

What does God's word say about arguing and quarreling?

Proverbs 15:1 says, "A soft answer turns away wrath, but a harsh word stirs up anger." Proverbs 20:3 goes on to say, "It is an honor for a man to keep aloof from strife, but every fool will be quarreling. Avoiding a fight is a mark of honor; only fools insist on quarreling."

This is a hard pill to swallow, for when we are hurt, we want the other person to feel the agonizing pain we feel. Our fleshly selves are often not satisfied unless we make sure that we inflict pain on our spouse that is far worse than what we are feeling at the moment. Isn't it intriguing how frequently we succumb to being led by our emotions even when they cause us to behave like absolute fools and simply aggravate the situation?

How does Jane's conduct need to change in order to be in line with God's word?

Strive for peace

Psalm 34:14 says, "Turn away from evil and do good; seek peace and pursue it." We should always promote and pursue peace with our spouse, especially when your spouse's actions clearly indicate that he or she is frustrated and angry. Being hurt does not give us permission to respond in a like manner. God calls us to change the dysfunctional interactional pattern by not participating in the spat but by doing the exact opposite, restoring the relationship through reconciliation and making every effort to promote unity versus division.

Confession

People often yearn to get even when they are hurt, as was the case with Jane. Thus, Jane's time of confession with the Lord could have focused on admitting her desire to settle the score with John and how this was more important to her than exhibiting love and working toward healthy resolution. She could have prayed for strength to prevent this unhealthy desire toward retaliation from being acted upon. Jane could have asked for the Lord's peace to permeate her heart and to be used as a vessel for peace in a situation filled with turmoil.

If Jane were to confess this to John, it could have opened up a time of discussion regarding her inclination to retaliate in like manner when she is hurt. She could have shared with John that her pattern of response is to hurt when she is hurt, the struggle she has with responding in love when she is hurt, and asked for his forgiveness.

Return good for evil

Proverbs 15:1 says, "A soft answer turns away wrath, but a harsh word stirs up anger." This verse points out how harsh words stir up friction and conflict. Hopefully by now you are getting the point that even when our spouse's actions do not convey the compassion and sensitivity we desire, it does not give us permission to respond in the same manner. Therefore, one way to diffuse anger is to respond in a loving, concerned, and considerate manner.

Knowing what Scripture says about stirring up discord with the words you utter, here are some ideas on how Jane could have handled her frustration in a more loving way:

- Instead of getting drawn into an argument, Jane could have tried to pursue peace with her incensed husband. Jane could have invited John to vent about his day without lambasting him with her words.

- Jane could have gently rubbed John's back and in a tender voice expressed that it seems as though they both had a rough day.

- Jane could have walked John over to a comfortable chair, encouraged him to sit and relax, and brought him a small snack and drink to hold him over until dinner was ready.

Self-reflection

The cause of arguing and quarreling is multi-factorial. Tim and Joy Downs (2010) highlighted seven potential root causes for recurring conflict: *security, loyalty, responsibility, caring, order, openness, and connection.* These serve as hot buttons that clue us in to specific issues that may result in noted frustration, disappointment, and a tendency to want to get in the ring with our spouse.

Let's apply this to Jane's case and see what hot buttons were pushed as a result of John's outburst. This situation may have caused Jane to be concerned about the issue of *security*, as her experience of the situation may have left her feeling as though her marriage was in jeopardy. *Loyalty* is another, as Jane may have perceived John's biting comments as though he was questioning her loyalty to him because of his perception that she was failing to tend to his needs. Yet another is *connection*, as Jane may have felt that her need for connection with John was threatened when he berated her rather than engaged her in conversation.

Whatever your hot button may be, it would be wise to become well-acquainted with what your sensitive areas are. Although the process is far from enjoyable, we need to make a concerted effort to examine these issues for ourselves and make time to discuss them as a couple. As we identify our sensitive areas, we can be better prepared to recognize our unhealthy response patterns, as well as prevent conflict from recurring.

Time for self-reflection

• Have I experienced the heart condition of arguing and

quarreling? If so, how do I respond?

- Knowing what God's word says about arguing and quarreling, what do I need to change in order to be in line with God's word?

Heart Condition: Envy That Leads to Discontentment and Bitterness

Many people view themselves as being "good." They do what they believe is morally right. They avoid doing things that would hurt others. They do their civic duty of voting. They donate to causes that help their community, and every Christmas they donate extra gifts to families who cannot afford them. Sounds like these folks do a lot of noble things to help their fellow man.

Nevertheless, have you ever desperately craved for something that you did not or could not have? If you answered "no" to this question, you may have to take an honest look at yourself and think a little harder. Have you ever looked at something your neighbor recently obtained and wished that you could have it too? Say, for example, that new home theater system that brings the theater experience to life in your very own home, or the custom inground swimming pool they just built? What about your coworker who bought a new car, the very one you've had your eye on with all the "bells and whistles" you could possibly imagine? What about the promotion you thought you were guaranteed to get that was given to your coworker instead? Or, what about the trip to the Bahamas your friends recently came back from that you have been dreaming of for the past decade?

We have all experienced discontentment, which is the yearning for something we do not have. This is a common occurrence even in marriages. Let's see how it played out in Ethan and Elaine's marriage.

Ethan and Elaine live next door to Mark and Mary whom they share a lot in common with. They are all about the same age, they both have two children around the same age, and Ethan and Mark both work outside of the home while their wives tend to the home and children. Over time the couples developed a rather close relationship. A few months ago, they started having family dinner nights twice a month and took turns hosting it at each other's home. Ethan began noticing that Mark and Mary's home was a lot neater and tidier, and that Mary always served an array of homemade food from appetizers, a delicious entrée, and delectable desserts. On the contrary, Ethan viewed his home as a disaster zone and found Elaine's cooking to be less than appealing, as she always served some form of casserole for dinner and whatever ice cream that was in the freezer for dessert. At first Ethan didn't think anything of it, but soon found himself wishing that their home was better organized and uncluttered, and that Elaine cooked a better selection of meals. Ethan eventually started nitpicking at Elaine about the condition of their home and her cooking. He began making disparaging remarks such as, "Why is the house always such a mess?" "Can't we eat anything other than a casserole every night?" "While I am out slaving away at work, what on earth do you do all day at home?" Elaine began feeling as though she was unable to do anything to please Ethan. She felt frustrated and started to withdraw from interacting with him, which contributed to increased friction in their marriage.

What does Ethan's response to the situation say about the condition of his heart?

Ethan's desire for things to be different is not inherently wrong, but what this story illustrates is that as Ethan started to compare what he had to others, envy began to well up in his heart. Consequently, he was no longer able to see his home and wife as blessings. Rather, he became discontent with the management of the household. Ethan's discontentment turned into bitterness that was then taken out on Elaine. Instead of addressing it with Elaine, his discontentment led him to become bitter and spiteful, and he started shifting blame for his own personal issue onto his wife.

What does God's word say about envy, discontentment, and bitterness?

Envy (or coveting) was discussed in Exodus 20:17, "You shall not covet your neighbor's house; you shall not covet your neighbor's wife, or his male servant, or his female servant, or his ox, or his donkey, or anything that is your neighbor's." Proverbs 14:30 addressed envy by saying, "A tranquil heart gives life to the flesh, but envy makes the bones rot." Envy is diametrically opposed to having a tranquil heart, as it leads to destruction that can manifest in various ways, one of which is the breakdown of a marriage.

When it comes to discontentment, 1 Timothy 6:6-7 says, "But godliness with contentment is great gain, for we brought nothing into the world, and we cannot take anything out of the world." Hebrews 13:5 goes on to say, "Keep your life free from love of money, and be content with what you have, for he has said, 'I will never leave you nor forsake you.'" When our attention is diverted from the countless ways that God has blessed us, we become vulnerable to being discontent and find ourselves constantly looking at other things to fulfill the needs that only God can. Furthermore, it renders us unable to see that joy and satisfaction can only be experienced when we learn to appreciate the blessings that God has put before us.

In regards to bitterness, Ephesians 4:31-32 says, "Let all bitterness and wrath and anger and clamor and slander be put away from you, along with all malice. Be kind to one another, tenderhearted, forgiving one another, as God in Christ forgave you." Hebrews 12:15 goes on to explain the effects of bitterness, "See to it that no one fails to obtain the grace of God; that no 'root of bitterness' springs up and causes trouble, and by it many become defiled." Bitterness is the antithesis of being kind, tenderhearted, and forgiving, and leads to a host of interpersonal problems.

How does Ethan's conduct need to change in order to be in line with God's word?

Focus on things of eternal value

When our eyes are fixed on the things of this world, we become more enticed by their perceived glitz and glamour regardless of the fact that they have no eternal value. Aside from tangible items like our possessions, things of the world include those things that fill our minds with an altered sense of self-importance, such as our career, position at work, socioeconomic class, social standing, membership in prestigious organizations, the number of social media followers you have, the number of likes you get on a post, etc. We can easily become mesmerized by these things and find ourselves on a constant pursuit for more of it.

Matthew 6:33 sums it up as it reads, "But seek first the kingdom of God and his righteousness, and all these things will be added to you." This can be done in your marriage. How? When our passion is to honor the Lord in all areas of our life and to see His kingdom expanded here on earth, the way we treat our spouse and our marriage is a reflection of the love we have for the Lord. By honoring your spouse through your conduct, actively taking steps each day to encourage your spouse, making an effort to learn more about your spouse's interests, finding ways to bless them, and allowing yourself to be vulnerable in the relationship so that you can take your marriage to a more intimate level, you will find that your spouse and marriage will never lose their luster because you have focused on something of eternal value.

Confession

When we allow envy, discontentment, and bitterness to become the dominant force behind our actions, we have in effect misplaced our trust in the things of this world to bring peace, security, comfort, satisfaction, and joy. In the process we render what God has blessed us with and what He is doing in our lives of little or no importance. Therefore, Ethan's time of confession could focus on asking for the Lord's forgiveness for his misplaced trust in temporary earthly things rather than in God and what is of eternal value. He could also pray that the Lord help to open his eyes to those things of eternal value that he has been blind to.

No one likes admitting fault or disclosing their areas of weakness, yet the only way a couple can draw closer is to put down their guard and allow their spouse to see all facets of their being and character if there is to be any hope of both partners being able to encourage and support one another in their time of need. Thus, it would be beneficial for Ethan to share with Elaine his propensity to seek comfort and satisfaction in the things of the world, and how his dissatisfaction ends up getting inappropriately directed at her.

Return good for evil

So, what could Ethan do now that he has inappropriately directed his discontentment with his circumstances to his wife?

- Clearly it is necessary for Ethan to shift what he has made his focal point. After confessing to Elaine and asking for her forgiveness, he can ask her to help him identify all the ways that the Lord has blessed him and the family so that he can verbally express them and reflect on them.

- Ethan may be at a total loss for how he can express love to Elaine in a way that she can receive it at that moment. So, he could tell Elaine that his desire is to move toward restoring their relationship and ask her what she thinks would be helpful. This would provide Ethan with the information he needs to take immediate action to help mend the relationship.

  If Elaine is too distraught to articulate what would be helpful in the moment, reestablishing a connection can be done through physical means, such as Ethan reaching out to hold Elaine's hand and even extending a comforting embrace.

- Sometimes couples struggle simply because their expectations have not been articulated. As a result, both parties end up functioning in the dark and can only hope that what they do meets or exceeds unknown or potentially unrealistic expectations. When both Ethan and Elaine have a chance to calm down and are in a position to receive feedback, Ethan could ask Elaine if they could set aside time to talk specifically about the clarification of expectations. He could extend some time to Elaine to have her share what her expectations are for the organization and functioning of the household.

  Once Elaine has had a chance to share her expectations, Ethan could initiate discussion by highlighting similar expectations that they both share and build upon them. This will allow them to talk about their own expectations, what they look like, see how they differ, whether they are realistic, and work to modify them so they are aligned with each other's.

Self-reflection

There is relational danger lurking around the corner when our hearts are consumed with envy, discontentment, and bitterness. The destruction starts in our hearts, as we become closed off to both the giving and receiving of love. This creates a significant barrier to the process of relational reconciliation. As the negative emotions associated with envy, discontentment, and bitterness (i.e., anger, resentment, etc.) increase and intensify within a person, it leaves one vulnerable to explosive emotional discharges. When a person reaches this point, engaging in the belittlement of others and making false and damaging accusations becomes a habitual pattern. The relational focus deviates from efforts to bond and extend love to wounding the very person you love. The envy, discontentment, and bitterness offender has a serious choice to make—allow this sin to consume them or to allow the love of Christ to restore them.

Time for self-reflection

- Have I experienced the heart condition of envy that leads to discontentment and bitterness? If so, how do I respond?

- Knowing what God's word says about envy, discontentment, and bitterness, what do I need to change in order to be in line with God's word?

Heart Condition:
Desire for Revenge

Many of us have seen movies where couples become upset with one another and then try to find ways to get back at the other. Some of these interactions are depicted in comedies. The antics of the couple are performed in such a humorous fashion that for a moment in time we easily overlook how such tactics breed a lack of trust and the inability to depend and rely on your spouse.

We have examined how emotional pain is exhibited in a host of harmful heart conditions. Since a marriage involves two distinct and vastly different individuals, the clash of the harmful heart conditions from both parties can be absolutely devastating to a marriage. Let's revisit Ethan and Elaine's story and continue on to see how Elaine handled things. Sadly, it is yet another illustration of the consequences of relational issues that are not properly resolved.

> *Ethan and Elaine live next door to Mark and Mary whom they share a lot in common with. They are all about the same age, they both have two children around the same age, and Ethan and Mark both work outside of the home while their wives tend to the home and children. Over time the couples developed a rather close relationship. A few months ago, they started having family dinner nights twice a month and took turns hosting it at each other's home. Ethan began noticing that Mark and Mary's home was a lot neater and tidier, and that Mary always served an array of homemade food from appetizers, a delicious entrée, and delectable desserts. On the contrary, Ethan viewed his home as a disaster zone and found Elaine's cooking to be less than appealing, as she always served some form of casserole for dinner and whatever ice cream that was in the freezer for dessert. At first Ethan didn't think anything of it, but soon found himself wishing that their home was better organized and uncluttered, and that Elaine cooked a better selection of meals. Ethan eventually started nitpicking at Elaine about the condition of their home and her cooking. He began making disparaging remarks such as, "Why is the house always such a mess?" "Can't we eat anything other than a casserole every night?" "While I am out slaving away at work, what on earth do you do all day at home?"*

Elaine began feeling as though she was unable to do anything to please Ethan. She felt frustrated and started to withdraw from interacting with him, which contributed to increased friction in their marriage.

Elaine found herself holding on to the pain that Ethan's spiteful remarks inflicted and began loathing his presence. When she could no longer contend with Ethan's unpleasant comments, Elaine vowed she would "teach him a lesson" so that he would never do that again. In a vengeful fit of rage, she emptied bags of trash inside Ethan's car at night while he was asleep. When he awoke the next morning, he was mortified to see the interior of his car covered in rubbish and rotting food.

In this real-life story, we see an unhealthy exchange taking place between a husband and wife that escalated and reflects the condition of the hearts of both parties. As we just looked at the condition of Ethan's heart, let's turn our attention to Elaine.

What does Elaine's response to the situation say about the condition of her heart?

We see how Elaine's heart became filled with revenge after numerous hurtful biting comments. While Ethan's conduct was clearly out of line and did not help matters, Elaine is responsible for how she deals with the emotions she experiences and her own conduct. We can understand why Ethan's insensitive statements pained her, but how did Elaine's act of revenge help build up her husband and strengthen her marriage?

What does God's word say about revenge?

1 Peter 3:9 says, "Do not repay evil for evil or reviling for reviling, but on the contrary, bless, for to this you were called, that you may obtain a blessing." Luke also adds in Chapter 6 Verses 27 to 28, "But I say to you who hear, Love your enemies, do good to those who hate you, bless those who curse you, pray for those who abuse you."

First off, your spouse should not be your enemy, so why insist on doing things that will turn your spouse into an adversary? It is understandable that containing our pain, frustration, and anger is an incredibly challenging thing to do when we are hurt. But God is calling on us to honor Him by blessing the person who has wronged you. While the world may encourage and justify revenge in a situation like this, God is calling Christians to bless the "offender" by making a conscious decision to restore the relationship.

How does Elaine's conduct need to change in order to be in line with God's word?

Forgiveness

Our initial response to being hurt is the desire to have the offender come begging on their hands and knees asking for forgiveness. However, Matthew 6:14 says, "For if you forgive others their trespasses, your heavenly Father will also forgive you." We are not called to wait for our offender to extend the olive branch signifying a desire for peace and reconciliation. No, that is actually *our* responsibility. God extends forgiveness to us when we are the ones who have sinned against Him. God is calling on us to do the same, to forgive others regardless of the extent to which we have been wounded.

In many cases this requires giving up the need to be right and the need to be vindicated. Rather than putting all of your effort into getting back at your spouse, put your energy into mending the relationship. If you know that forgiveness is the essential piece in the puzzle that will help to restore a damaged relationship, it seems quite absurd to allow your pride to get in the way of your own personal healing and that of the relationship.

Confession

When a person gets to the point of thinking about and/or engaging in vengeful acts, it means that they have been storing up their pain and keeping a record of the times they have been mistreated. Rather than relinquishing their emotional distress and putting it all before the feet of Jesus, the offender clings to it in hopes that it can be used in the future against the perpetrator.

Therefore, Elaine's confession could focus on the fact that she did not act in a loving way, for "Love is patient and kind; love does not envy or boast; it is not arrogant or rude. It does not insist on its own way; it is not irritable or resentful; it does not rejoice at wrongdoing, but rejoices with the truth. Love bears all things, believes all things, hopes all things, endures all things" (1 Corinthians 13:4-7).

She could confess that she allowed her resentment to build up rather than exercising forgiveness. She could pray for the Lord's strength to ward off the painful, fiery darts thrown her way, and for pride to be removed from her heart so that she is inclined to respond in love even when she simply wants to retaliate.

Return good for evil

Although our thoughts, feelings, and behaviors are under our control, we often let them take control of us in emotionally-heated situations. This in turn leads to unhealthy/inappropriate decisions and conduct. Here are some things that Elaine could have done in this situation:

- Elaine could have chosen to exercise forgiveness, which obviously is preferable when you look at things with spiritual eyes. It is easy to remain resentful towards someone who has hurt you, but we must remember to see our spouse as God does: someone whom He has created and loves.

- Elaine could have taken some time to go to the Lord in prayer and ask for guidance and wisdom on how to talk to Ethan about how she has been feeling so that her words would be seasoned with grace versus being confrontational.

- From there, Elaine could schedule a time to talk with Ethan to prevent distractions and interruptions. Without other things vying for their attention, she could speak to him in a rational and calm manner about what she has observed, which is how important it is to him that the house look a certain way.

Prior to the conversation, Elaine could pray for strength and for the Holy Spirit to empower her not to take any of Ethan's criticisms as an attack on who she is, as the issue is the orderliness of the household and not Elaine herself (which is what she is responding to).

By allowing Ethan the opportunity to verbalize his expectations and what this means in their household, she is intentionally making a conscientious effort to convey that she cares about what he thinks. It also helps Elaine develop a better understanding of what it is about their current situation that Ethan finds so distasteful. Until she knows exactly what that is, there is no opportunity for any kind of change to be made.

As they talk about his expectations, they can determine whether such expectations are realistic based on their unique circumstances. This may mean that Ethan and/or Elaine will have to alter their expectations. But without having some kind of dialogue about the situation, both parties are left feeling unappreciated, resentful, and angry. Ethan may not realize just how hurtful his comments are. As Elaine calmly and gently expresses how she feels in response to Ethan's comments, he is made aware of the negative impact they have on his wife, the person whom he is supposed to love as Christ loved the church and gave Himself up for her (Ephesians 5:25), and whom he should not be harsh toward (Colossians 3:19).

Self-reflection

Regardless of whether we are the offended or the offender, we need to continuously check the condition of our hearts to ensure that we do not aggravate a challenging situation. Each of us is responsible for our thoughts, feelings, and behaviors. All three of these things are under our control. Unfortunately, we often allow ourselves to be taken captive by our thoughts and feelings.

2 Corinthians 10:5 says, "We destroy arguments and every lofty opinion raised against the knowledge of God, and take every thought captive to obey Christ." If we are honest, we all can say that there has been at least one instance in our lives when we made decisions or acted in ways that we thought were right

in our own minds and put that before what God calls us to do in emotionally-heated situations. However, we need to remember that it is within our power to make the choice to bless the person who hurt us by not allowing things to escalate. We can make a conscious decision to put the marriage and the other person first and be the one to initiate taking steps to restore the relationship.

This is not the first thing we think about when we are wronged. But then again, who said that Christians should resolve difficulties in ways that are akin to that of the world?

Time for self-reflection

- Have I experienced the heart condition of revenge? If so, how do I respond?

- Knowing what God's word says about revenge, what do I need to change in order to be in line with God's word?

Heart Condition: Lying

In case it hasn't been stressed enough, it is important to know that our hearts are desperately wicked. We all want to believe that we are "good" people. In fact, many behavioral theorists believe that we are born good. Conversely, we see from parenting that most of the time spent with children is focused on teaching them how to behave properly as it is their innate tendency to engage in selfish conduct. If you don't believe this, then ask yourself why must we teach them to share and to help others? Why must we teach children not to lie?

Jeremiah 17:9 says, "The heart is deceitful above all things, and desperately wicked: who can know it?"

Humans struggle with being truthful, for telling the truth can lead to unfavorable consequences. Be that as it may, no one wants to be perceived as a liar. In fact, society has tried to "normalize" lying by creating distinctions between a "bold-faced lie" and a "white lie" probably for this very reason. It seems as though society wants to adopt the notion that if your intentions are "honorable," then lying to achieve a virtuous goal is deemed to be acceptable. On the other hand, lying to cover up one's actions or to simply get what you want is objectionable.

What do you think? Perhaps looking at the story of Bruce and Betty will shed some light on this matter:

> *Bruce had such a busy day at work that he did not get a chance to eat lunch. On his way home, he got caught in traffic. Although his wife Betty always has dinner ready when he arrives home from work, he was so hungry that he decided to stop at a drive-through restaurant and grab something quick to eat rather than sit in traffic. Bruce was famished and ended up eating more than he expected. When he got home, Betty greeted him with a big smile, as she was excited to share that she prepared his favorite meal. Bruce felt absolutely terrible and couldn't bring himself to tell her that he was so hungry that he had already eaten. He realized all the effort she went through to make his favorite dish and didn't want to hurt her feelings. So, Bruce thanked her for making the meal, but said he wasn't hungry because he wasn't feeling well.*

What does Bruce's response to the situation say about the condition of his heart?

Was there really any infraction that took place here? Some

people would say, "What's the big deal? Bruce didn't *totally* lie. He did say that he wasn't hungry, which was true." Some would argue that there was a kernel of truth in Bruce's comment, and others would say that it's better to tell a "white lie" than see your spouse's feelings get hurt.

Nevertheless, whatever explanation you come up with, the bottom line is that Bruce made a conscious choice to lie rather than tell the truth to prevent having a negative interaction with his wife. No one likes negative interactions or hurting a loved one's feelings, and so we often justify doing whatever we can to prevent adverse situations from occurring—even if it means telling a lie.

What does God's word say about lying?

Let's first think about who is the father of lies? As Christians, we know that to be Satan. And as Christians, aren't we called to bend our will to that of God's versus our own, or Satan's, regardless of the situation?

In John 8:44, he describes the enemy in these words, "You are of your father the devil, and your will is to do your father's desires. He was a murderer from the beginning, and does not stand in the truth, because there is no truth in him. When he lies, he speaks out of his own character, for he is a liar and the father of lies."

So, if you are willing to lie, what does that say about your character? What does that say about the condition of your heart? Telling the truth can be painful for you and for your spouse to hear. At the same time, lying does nothing but dishonors God, dishonors your spouse, and creates a fracture in the marital bond. If you are able to justify lying in a situation like Bruce's, could this lead to lying about other issues?

Proverbs 12:22 says, "Lying lips are an abomination to the

Lord, but those who act faithfully are his delight."

Therefore, let our lips glorify the Lord by speaking truth, even in those hard situations.

How does Bruce's conduct need to change in order to be in line with God's word?

Be truthful

While this seems obvious, being truthful can be hard for some when avoiding the fear of an unfavorable result becomes of greater importance than adherence to God's word. As mentioned previously in Proverbs 12:22, "Lying lips are an abomination to the LORD, but those who act faithfully are his delight." It is time that we start saying no to gratifying our own selfish desires and take up our cross (Matthew 16:24-26) if we really desire to follow after Christ.

Confession

A willingness to lie is a reflection of our desire to take the easy route that prevents us from experiencing any discomfort, even if it means disregarding God's word when it comes to valuing honesty and integrity. Thus, Bruce's confession should focus on asking for the Lord's forgiveness for elevating himself over striving for godly obedience and saying no to fleshly desires. Bruce could also pray for strength to strive for being transparent in his relationship with his wife rather than allowing himself to become desensitized to justifying lying.

Obviously in this situation, Bruce's confession to his wife is the crux of the matter. While it is true that Betty may not respond favorably to his honest comment, she will know that her husband can be trusted to be truthful in even what is deemed to be "minor" things.

Return good for evil

Lying tarnishes the level of trust our spouse has in us. If our ultimate goal in a relationship is to see it flourish, we need to seek restoration through confession and making an effort to exhibit love when we engage in conduct that can lead to relational distress. Bruce could have done this through any of the following examples:

- After confessing his sin to Betty, Bruce could have taken responsibility for his actions and asked for her forgiveness.

- Bruce could have taken the time to express his feelings by sharing how grateful he is for Betty's heart and that she thinks of different ways to lift his spirits, like making his favorite meal.

  Being grateful for how she blessed him with his favorite meal, Bruce could take it with him to work the following day and enjoy the meal for lunch. As he enjoys his lunch, he could take selfies of himself savoring every bite and send them to Betty as a way to show his appreciation, and hopefully the pictures will bring a smile to her face.

- Bruce could have gently and lovingly shared with his wife how challenging his day was and how he missed eating lunch, but that it would bring him joy to sit at the table with her as she enjoyed his favorite meal for him and talk about how she prepared it.

- Bruce could initiate a plan to notify Betty no later than

1:30 p.m. on days when he doesn't get a chance to eat lunch, and also inform her if he stops off at a restaurant on the way home to get a quick bite. Notifying her early enough will prevent her from preparing too large of a meal or something that will take a number of hours to prepare.

Self-reflection

If you have found yourself stuck in a web of lies, it is not too late to change things. God does extend forgiveness of our sins. This is not to say that there aren't consequences for our actions. However, if God is able to save us from the penalty of sin, He is more than capable of helping us change our lying ways if we fully surrender our will to Him. Let Him restore you and allow the words you utter to be those that refresh others and venerate Him.

Time for self-reflection

- Have I experienced the heart condition of lying? If so, how do I respond?

- Knowing what God's word says about lying, what do I need to change in order to be in line with God's word?

Conclusion

Hopefully you have picked up on the importance of seeking restoration of the relationship, as this is in line with what God has done for us by extending His forgiveness when we sinned against Him, a second chance we clearly didn't deserve. First Corinthians Chapter 13 Verse 5 in the New International Version translation of the Bible says that love "keeps no record of wrongs." That is exactly what Christ did for us. By giving Himself as a ransom for our sins, He wiped our slates clean of the sins of the past, present, and future. This is the very same thing we are called to do in our marriages. We must love our spouse and extend forgiveness regardless of whether you think it is warranted or not.

What? How could I suggest such an outrageous thing? Our flesh has no desire to forgive others when we are hurt unless it is deserved. We would much rather wallow in our pain and direct that negative emotion toward our spouse. But it is that very kind of thinking that perpetuates a vicious cycle of being driven by the condition of our heart and negative emotions rather than the love that God calls us to exhibit toward our spouse and others.

Is it hard? Absolutely! Are you going to struggle? Yes, there's no question about it! Are you going to fail? Yes, from time to time. Is it worth it? YES!

At the beginning of this book I disclosed that I am an absolute failure at keeping plants alive. I also shared what was at the root of the issue (no pun intended). It's not that I am simply inept at keeping plants alive. The reason for my ineptitude is that I was not invested in caring for the plants. I simply did not care enough to take the time to learn what was necessary to keep them alive. Because I didn't care, all the plants I had died.

This can be applied to marriage as well. If you don't care to invest in your marriage, it *will* die. We can come up with a ton of excuses for why we either can't or shouldn't put the effort into the relationship. But with every excuse we give, we end up creating more distance between us and our spouse and developing a heart that is more callous and uncaring. As a result, we lose the motivation to learn how to connect with our spouse, and the relationship withers and dies.

Just as a plant requires constant attention and tending to, so does a marriage. There are a number of issues that spring up like weeds in a marriage. Weeds come in all shapes and sizes. The extent of damage they can do can be anticipated, but if left unattended, they can be noxious and choke the lifeblood out of a marriage. This is why we have to be attentive to looking for those conditions of the heart that get in the way of us desiring the best for our spouse and our marriage.

Take a look at the impact of what happens when a wife is hurt and becomes emotionally and physically distant. In Ethan and Elaine's situation, we saw how the emotional anguish Elaine experienced fueled the desire to get revenge on her husband. She did so by dumping garbage in Ethan's car. She gave no thought to the ramifications of her conduct or to the fact that despite it being the car Ethan uses, it was still *their* car that belonged to *their* family that she was destroying.

Sadly, in this real-life example, Ethan returned evil for evil and took his revenge out on Elaine by distancing himself and engaging in an affair. It wasn't until their hearts seemed broken beyond repair that they realized that they were walking on thin ice and finally mustered up the courage to ask for help.

You may have gone through this book and failed to successfully implement these concepts in your marriage. You may be wondering if this is an indication that your marriage is over and cannot be resuscitated. Absolutely not! In actuality, if you have thoroughly gone through this material and taken the time to identify your "weeds" (the condition of your heart), you are in a better place to evaluate the conflict that is entrenched in your heart that is negatively impacting your ability to love your spouse as Jesus is calling us to. You may simply need additional help from someone who is trained to help couples move beyond the obstacles that heart conditions can have on a marriage. I implore you to consider speaking with your pastor or a trained professional who can provide proper biblical guidance on relationship matters.

Each of the couples in these examples sought out help because they recognized that they were unable to restore the relationship on their own. By examining what was leading to the growth of the "weeds" in their marriage and the condition of each of their hearts, we were able to get to the root of the matter (once again, no pun intended) and work to prevent the patterns from continuously being repeated.

Although we often prefer what is predictable over the unknown, repeating the same unhealthy patterns drains couples of the energy they need to invest in the marriage. We each need to do everything possible to take the steps that are required to restore the relationship. That means relying on God's word as our guide versus our own thoughts and emotions. That means we have to take our spouse into consideration whenever we make a decision, for we do not function independently or in our own little bubble. That means taking a risk and doing things that require us to go outside our comfort zone because the marital bond is at stake. And, that means being willing to go the extra mile even when we don't get the response we want in return.

A friend, Pastor Frank Figueroa Jr., reminded me that Jesus loved us 100% even when we loved Him 0%. This is reflected in Romans 5:6-10, "For while we were still weak, at the right time Christ died for the ungodly. For one will scarcely die for a righteous person—though perhaps for a good person one would dare even to die—but God shows His love for us in that while we were still sinners, Christ died for us. Since, therefore, we have now been justified by His blood, much more shall we be saved by Him from the wrath of God. For if while we were enemies we were reconciled to God by the death of His Son, much more, now that we are reconciled, shall we be saved by His life."

Jesus's love for us was not dependent on how much we loved Him. He did not create a set of conditions for us to meet before He would consider dying on the cross for us. Nor does He stop loving us whenever we make mistakes. This concept of unconditional love is foreign in today's societal climate because making sacrifices of any sort, whether that be of our time, energy, and/or resources, is frowned upon unless there is a clear expectation of getting something in return.

The word "sacrifice" is deemed to be so objectionable because of what it requires—giving of ourselves without expectation of anything in return. Our society has conditioned us to act in a manner that is self-serving and focused on self-gratification. As a result, we have become inept at putting the needs of others before ourselves. Nevertheless, there is no possible way for a relationship to grow if our focus is on our own personal interests.

Just as Jesus's love for us was not dependent on whether we

loved Him, our love for our spouse should not be dependent on whether they are loving toward us. In fact, if we use Jesus as an example of how to love our spouse, we are to love them 100% no matter what—even if they are acting in a hurtful and spiteful manner.

I recognize that for some of you this may seem inconceivable because of what you have experienced, but marriage is not about getting love from another person, although that is what we all desire. Marriage is about making a conscious choice to love a person regardless of who they are or what the circumstances may be. This is the very thing that Jesus has done for us.

Plants will only grow as much as they are tended to and cared for. Marriage is no different. And, just as you need to regularly manage weeds in a garden, addressing matters of the heart is an ongoing, lifelong process that is necessary for the health and vitality of your marriage. Therefore, kill the noxious weeds before they take over and choke the lifeblood out of your marriage! Tend to your spouse and to your marriage by giving it 100% of your attention, 100% of your energy, and 100% of your love, and watch it flourish!

References

Brody, J. E. (2007). "Out of Control: A True Story of Binge Eating." Retrieved from https://www.nytimes.com/2007/02/20/health/20brod.html

Dockray, H. (2015). "You Can't Win That Facebook Fight." Retrieved from https://mashable.com/2015/11/07/why-you-cant-win-facebook-fight/#GEg5u8qBPGqg

Downs, T. & J. (2010). "Why Do We Keep Arguing?" Retrieved from https://www.familylife.com/articles/topics/marriage/staying-married/resolving-conflict/why-do-we-keep-arguing

Hubbard, G. (2003). *Don't Make Me Count to Three! A Mom's Look at Heart-Oriented Discipline.* Wapwallopen, PA: Shepherd Press.

Lane, S. (2014). "The 10 Most Passive-Aggressive Things You're Doing on Social Media." Retrieved from https://mashable.com/2014/06/27/social-media-passive-aggressive/#X2nwo1bV4aqm

McLeod, L. (2018). "How to Deal With the 5 Most Negative Types of Co-Workers." Retrieved from https://www.themuse.com/advice/how-to-deal-with-the-5-most-negative-types-of-coworkers

Neighmond, P. (2011). "Road Rage: A Symptom of Much More Than Bad Traffic?" Retrieved from https://www.npr.org/sections/health-shots/2011/12/12/143457950/road-rage-a-symptom-of-much-more-than-bad-traffic

Sorgen, C. (2018). "Anger Management: Counting to 10 and Beyond." Retrieved from https://www.webmd.com/sex-relationships/features/anger-management-counting-to-ten#1

About the Author

Lei Ross, PsyD has a doctoral degree in Clinical Psychology and practiced for several years until her "Damascus Road" experience that radically transformed her into a follower of Jesus Christ. Since then, her study of Scripture has helped her reconcile observational psychological research with the Word of God which has given her a deeper understanding of human behavior. She and her husband of 25 years are passionate about promoting the joy of biblical marriage and formed the "Beyond Saying I Do" marriage ministry where they provide premarital/marital counseling, marital resources, and dating advice. She also volunteers as the prayer coordinator at her local church.

With a great affinity for French cuisine and architecture, Lei enjoys spending her free time researching and tasting chocolate, particularly 100% cacao, experimenting with French recipes, and feasting on French pastries. Aside from good French cuisine, she is fond of car shows like the original *Top Gear* and *The Grand Tour*. It is her dream to attend a real race, like the Formula 1 Monaco Grand Prix, but until then, she is content with watching it from the comfort of her own living room.

Addressing Matters of My Heart:
A Self-Reflection Journal

Date the situation occurred:

Describe the situation:

How did you respond?

What does your response to the situation say about the condition of your heart? (Refer to the chapter "How To Use This Book" for a list of heart conditions)

What does Scripture say about your heart condition?

(List and summarize the relevant Scripture verses)

How does your conduct need to change in order to be in line with God's word?

- Change related to the specific heart condition
  Scripture tells us how to address our heart conditions. Remember that God is calling us to do the exact opposite of the sinful heart condition (e.g., the change required for a heart consumed with anger is to be slow to anger).

- Confession
  (Take a moment to write out a confession. Acknowledge your sin and confess it to the Lord. Ask for His help to diminish the power that your sin has on your response patterns).

- Return good for evil
  (It is not anyone else's responsibility to change but your own, so do not focus on the response of others but on your own. Determine what steps you need to take to restore the relationship).

What have I learned as a result of identifying my heart condition and response

pattern? What do I need to do to apply this to my life?

Date the situation occurred:

Describe the situation:

How did you respond?

What does your response to the situation say about the condition of your heart? (Refer to the chapter "How To Use This Book" for a list of heart conditions)

What does Scripture say about your heart condition?

(List and summarize the relevant Scripture verses)

How does your conduct need to change in order to be in line with God's word?

- Change related to the specific heart condition
  Scripture tells us how to address our heart conditions. Remember that God is calling us to do the exact opposite of the sinful heart condition (e.g., the change required for a heart consumed with anger is to be slow to anger).

- Confession
  (Take a moment to write out a confession. Acknowledge your sin and confess it to the Lord. Ask for His help to diminish the power that your sin has on your response patterns).

- Return good for evil
  (It is not anyone else's responsibility to change but your own, so do not focus on the response of others but on your own. Determine what steps you need to take to restore the relationship).

What have I learned as a result of identifying my heart condition and response

pattern? What do I need to do to apply this to my life?

Date the situation occurred:

Describe the situation:

How did you respond?

What does your response to the situation say about the condition of your heart? (Refer to the chapter "How To Use This Book" for a list of heart conditions)

What does Scripture say about your heart condition?

(List and summarize the relevant Scripture verses)

How does your conduct need to change in order to be in line with God's word?

- Change related to the specific heart condition
  Scripture tells us how to address our heart conditions. Remember that God is calling us to do the exact opposite of the sinful heart condition (e.g., the change required for a heart consumed with anger is to be slow to anger).

- Confession
  (Take a moment to write out a confession. Acknowledge your sin and confess it to the Lord. Ask for His help to diminish the power that your sin has on your response patterns).

- Return good for evil
  (It is not anyone else's responsibility to change but your own, so do not focus on the response of others but on your own. Determine what steps you need to take to restore the relationship).

What have I learned as a result of identifying my heart condition and response

pattern? What do I need to do to apply this to my life?

Date the situation occurred:

Describe the situation:

How did you respond?

What does your response to the situation say about the condition of your heart? (Refer to the chapter "How To Use This Book" for a list of heart conditions)

What does Scripture say about your heart condition?

(List and summarize the relevant Scripture verses)

How does your conduct need to change in order to be in line with God's word?

- Change related to the specific heart condition
  Scripture tells us how to address our heart conditions. Remember that God is calling us to do the exact opposite of the sinful heart condition (e.g., the change required for a heart consumed with anger is to be slow to anger).

- Confession
  (Take a moment to write out a confession. Acknowledge your sin and confess it to the Lord. Ask for His help to diminish the power that your sin has on your response patterns).

- Return good for evil
  (It is not anyone else's responsibility to change but your own, so do not focus on the response of others but on your own. Determine what steps you need to take to restore the relationship).

What have I learned as a result of identifying my heart condition and response

pattern? What do I need to do to apply this to my life?

Date the situation occurred:

Describe the situation:

How did you respond?

What does your response to the situation say about the condition of your heart? (Refer to the chapter "How To Use This Book" for a list of heart conditions)

What does Scripture say about your heart condition?

(List and summarize the relevant Scripture verses)

How does your conduct need to change in order to be in line with God's word?

- Change related to the specific heart condition
  Scripture tells us how to address our heart conditions. Remember that God is calling us to do the exact opposite of the sinful heart condition (e.g., the change required for a heart consumed with anger is to be slow to anger).

- Confession
  (Take a moment to write out a confession. Acknowledge your sin and confess it to the Lord. Ask for His help to diminish the power that your sin has on your response patterns).

- Return good for evil
  (It is not anyone else's responsibility to change but your own, so do not focus on the response of others but on your own. Determine what steps you need to take to restore the relationship).

What have I learned as a result of identifying my heart condition and response

pattern? What do I need to do to apply this to my life?

www.ingramcontent.com/pod-product-compliance
Lightning Source LLC
Chambersburg PA
CBHW071136280326
41935CB00010B/1254